fun origami for children

Flight!

12 paper planes and other flying objects to fold for fun!

Mari Ono & Roshin Ono

CICO **Kidz**

Published in 2018 by CICO Books
An imprint of Ryland Peters & Small Ltd
20–21 Jockey's Fields   341 E 116th St
London WC1R 4BW   New York, NY 10029

www.rylandpeters.com

10 9 8 7 6 5 4 3 2 1

Text © Mari Ono and Roshin Ono 2018
Design and photography © CICO Books 2018

A CIP catalog record for this book is
available from the Library of Congress
and the British Library.

ISBN: 978 1 78249 579 6

Printed in China

Editor: Dawn Bates
Designer: Eliana Holder
Photographer: Geoff Dann
Art director: Sally Powell
Head of production: Patricia Harrington
Publishing manager: Penny Craig
Publisher: Cindy Richards

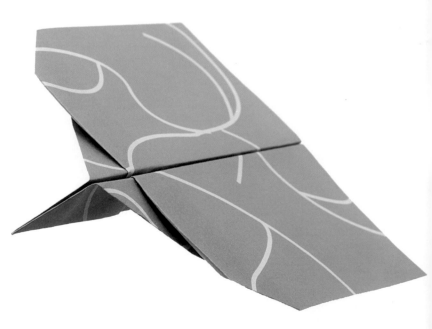

Contents

Welcome to Origami!

These fun paper planes and other flying objects have been designed for you to make by yourself or with a grown-up if you prefer. Begin with a simple project and learn a few basic folds before moving on to something a bit more ambitious.

You'll soon find yourself picking up the skills that Japanese people have been using for centuries, and making models that even origami masters would be proud of. Origami is great fun and we hope you will enjoy bringing the models to life.

Key to arrows

Fold
Fold the part of the paper shown in this direction.

Folding direction
Fold the entire paper over in this direction.

Open out
Open out and refold the paper over in the direction shown.

Change the position
Spin the paper 90° in the direction of the arrows.

Change the position
Spin the paper through 180°.

Turn over
Turn the paper over.

Make a crease
Fold the paper over in the direction of the arrow, then open it out again.

Look for the symbols!

 A good project to start with

 Move on to level 2

Perfect your skills with level 3

Basic Techniques

Origami is a very simple craft that only requires a steady hand and some patience. Before you start making your first model, just check over these simple tips to ensure every paper model you make is a success.

Making folds Making the paper fold as crisply and evenly as possible is the key to making models that will stand up as the designs intend—it really is as simple as that.

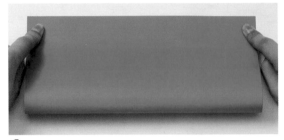

1 When you make a fold ensure that the paper lies exactly where you want it, with the corners sitting exactly on top of each other.

2 As you make the crease, be sure to keep the paper completely still so that the fold is straight.

3 Use a ruler or perhaps the side of a pencil to press down the fold until it is as flat as possible.

Opening folds

Sometimes you will need to open out a crease and refold the paper so that it lies in a new shape, as in the triangle fold shown here.

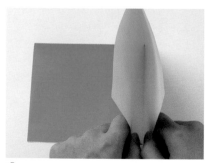  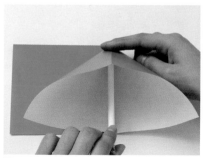 

1 Lift the flap to be opened out and begin pulling the two sides apart.

2 As the space widens you will need to be sure that the far point folds correctly, so use a pencil to gently prise the paper open.

3 As the two corners separate, the top point drops forward and the two edges open out to become one.

4 Press down the new creases to make the two new angled sides of the triangle.

Reversing folds

To reverse a crease you will need to open out your model and gently turn part of the paper back on itself. This can be tricky so practice on a spare piece of paper first.

  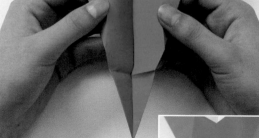 

1 To turn the tip back on itself, first make a firm crease with a simple fold.

2 Return the tip back to its original position and open out the model. Turn back the nose again along the fold you just made.

3 When you close the model together again, the tip has reversed and is now flat.

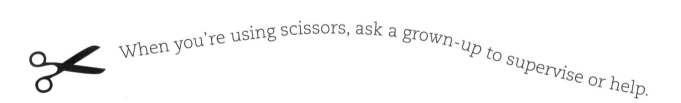

When you're using scissors, ask a grown-up to supervise or help.

Flying School

All the planes in this book will fly, though there are different ways to launch them. If you and your friends perfect your technique, you can have great competitions! Follow the instructions on these pages and then practice to achieve a long flight. Experiment by making small adjustments to the angle of the wings to help the plane fly straighter or higher.

Planes

Many of the planes are folded so that they have central bodies. Always check your creases are sharp and the paper is smooth before you throw it. Grip the plane between your thumb and forefinger to launch.

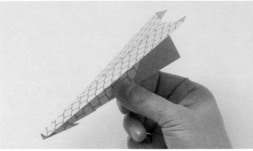

Classic plane–page 8

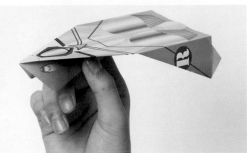

Ross-17–page 22

Into the air

To achieve really long flights, it can be helpful to throw the model high into the air. Use as much power as you can and practice to find the angle that works best.

1 Start by holding the plane low next to your ankles, with your knees bent.

2 As you raise the plane, lift your body.

3 Point the plane high into the sky and swivel your body to gain as much power as possible when you let go.

Throwing wings

When a plane does not have a body to grasp, it is more difficult to launch a significant distance. However, all of them will fly with a flick of the wrist.

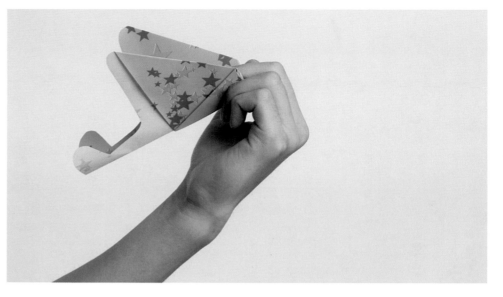

1 Grip the front of the plane from underneath with the tips of your fingers.

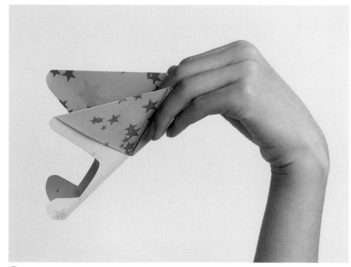

2 Flick your hand forward from the wrist to launch it.

3 Ensure your fingers end up pointing in the direction you want the plane to fly.

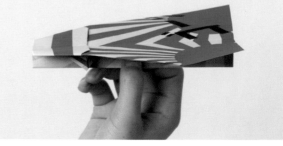

Classic Plane

Origami has been one of the most popular forms of play for Japanese children for centuries. The secrets of the art have been handed down from one generation to another, ensuring that the designs flourished. This classic paper airplane is a model that has always been much loved because it is so quick and easy to fold, and it flies very well.

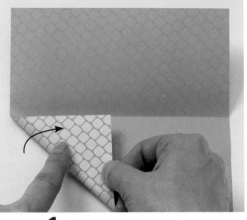

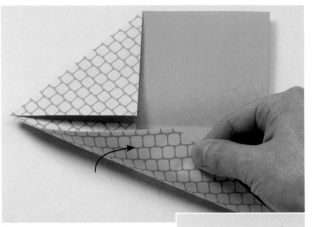

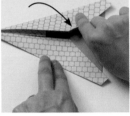

1 Make a crease down the center of the 10in (25cm) square paper by folding it in half, then opening it out. Turn in the corners of one end so that the sides lie along the central crease with the corners next to each other.

2 Fold the new edges in so that they also meet along the central crease of the paper.

3 Turn back the nose, folding it about 1¼in (3cm) from the end, then turn the object over and close up the plane along the original crease line.

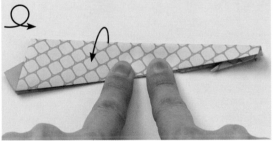

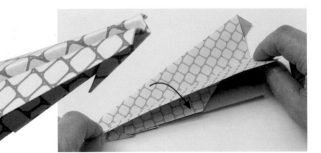

4 Turn over the wing at a slight angle so that the plane's body is deeper at the back than the front.

5 Turn the plane over and fold down the other wing so that it exactly matches the first, then open out the wings so that they sit together, at right angles to the body.

Pioneers! The Wright Brothers launched the world's first airplane in 1903.

Glider

Once you've made your classic plane, this simple glider is a great one to move on to. It is a cinch to make and is a brilliant flyer. With a gentle throw it will glide far and long, putting some of the more technical planes to shame. The trick is the double fold on the nose; it adds a bit of weight and helps it to go that extra bit farther.

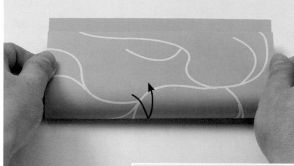

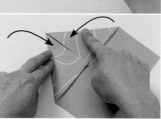

1 Fold the 10in (25cm) square paper in half and open it out to make a crease. Turn in the corners at one end so that they meet along the center crease.

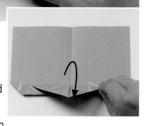

2 Fold back the nose, making the crease about 2in (5cm) inside the folds made in the previous step, then fold it back on itself, making the crease about 1in (2.5cm) from the first fold.

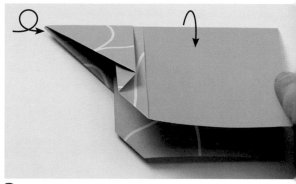

3 Turn the whole paper over and fold the object in half along the central crease.

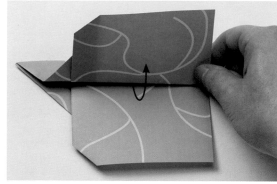

4 Turn back the top wing making the fold parallel to, and approximately 2in (5cm) up from, the bottom of the glider. Turn the model over and repeat on the other side.

5 Add a dab of glue inside the body of the glider and press together to ensure the two wings sit together.

Smooth ride! The record distance for hang-gliding is 475 miles (764km).

Star Strike

This airplane is designed to fly fast and far, resembling a comet hurtling through outer space. Try playing with the Star Strike indoors in a large room, throwing it high into the air toward the ceiling where it can fly before gliding gracefully back down to earth. See pages 6–7 for some useful tips on flying techniques.

 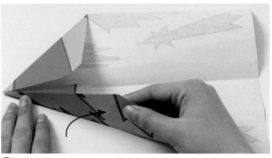 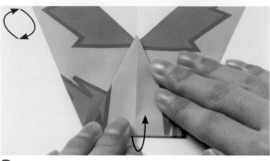

1 Fold the paper in half lengthways and open out to leave a crease, then fold in the corners at one end to meet along the center line.

2 Fold in the angled edges so that they also meet along the central crease line.

3 Spin the paper round and fold back the tip, ensuring that the tip just covers the point where the diagonal edges meet in the center.

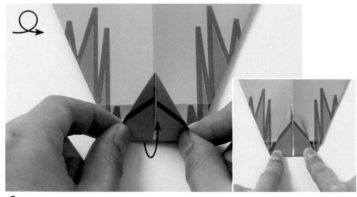 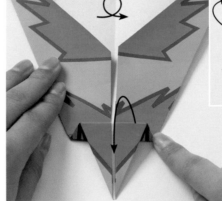 

4 Turn the paper over and open out the nose before folding it back on itself, making a crease approximately 2in (5cm) from the end.

5 Turn the paper back over and fold up the nose using the two creases just made, then spin the object and fold it together along the central crease.

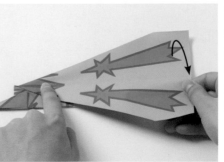

6 Fold down the wings with creases parallel to the base of the plane at the closest possible point to the nose.

Supersonic! It took Concorde just 3½ hours to fly from New York to Paris.

Star Light

In Japan this is called the "Swallow Plane," as it closely resembles the bird's swooping shape and flies with the same easy style. It does not have a body like most paper planes and flies in a unique way (see page 7). Although this method looks a little awkward at first, with practice the Star Light will fly as well as any plane.

1 First, fold the paper in half lengthwise and open out to make a crease. Next fold the corners of one end across to the other side of the paper, opening both out to make diagonal creases.

2 Fold the right-hand end of the paper over, using the crossing point of the diagonal creases as the marker for the fold.

3 Fold the corners into the center using the diagonal creases made earlier as the fold lines.

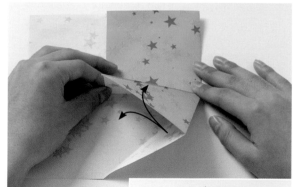

4 Open out the last folds and lift the nearest corner, taking it across to the other side of the paper so that the flap opens out before refolding it to form a triangle.

5 Fold the far point of the triangle back over to the near side of the object.

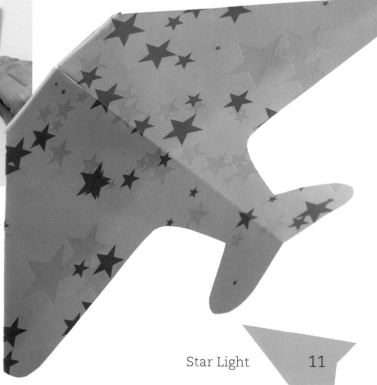

6 Lift the far point, opening out the flap and folding it toward you, forming another triangle.

7 Fold the top flap back over so that there is one flap on each side of the object.

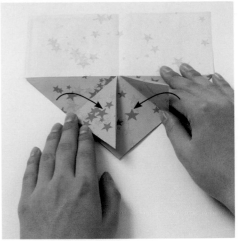

8 Fold the corners of both top flaps over so that the corners meet at the object's end point.

9 Fold the sides of the central diamond across the center so that they meet along the center line.

10 Lift the paper and use scissors to cut along the center line from the tip to the point at which the two folds made in the last step meet.

Let's fly! In the US there are around 29,000 flights each day.

11 Lift the top flaps and gently open them out with a finger or a pencil, then turn back each side of the nose and tuck them into the holes until the crease is flush.

12 Turn the object over and fold it in half along the central crease.

13 Use the scissors to cut out the shape of the wings and tail.

Thunderstorm

With its large wing span, the exciting Thunderstorm plane will fly far and true if you throw it with a bit of power up toward the sky, slicing quickly through the air.

Follow the steps carefully, to ensure that you turn over the nose just enough so that the wings sit together without the need for any glue.

1 Fold the paper in half to make a crease, then open it out again. Fold in the corners at one end to meet along the center line and then repeat, folding the angled sides so that they meet in the middle.

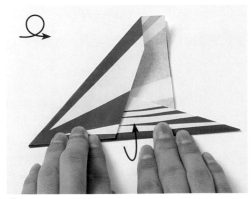

2 Fold back the end of the plane, making a crease about 5in (12.5cm) from the rear of the object.

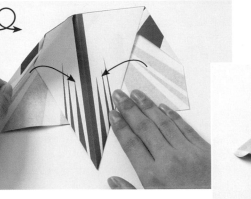

3 Turn the paper over and fold the back edges of the plane forward, angled so that they meet along the center line.

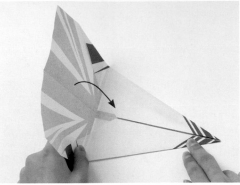

4 Turn the object over and fold it in half along the central crease.

Huge! The world's largest airplane has a wingspan of 385 feet (117 meters).

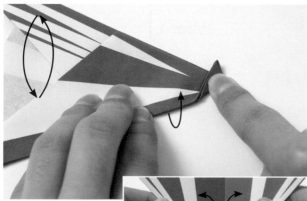

6 Gently reverse the creases made when you turned over the nose and push the object back together so that the nose now points downward.

5 Spin the object round and fold the tip of the nose across the main crease line, then open out the paper.

7 Fold the wings down, making the creases parallel to the bottom of the plane and starting just behind the turned nose.

Sunlight

One of the fastest and most stable airplane designs, the Sunlight's wide wing cuts through the wind, allowing it to fly straight and true, covering a good distance. Extend the duration of the flight even further by throwing it high up into the air (see page 6). You can use a larger sheet of rectangular paper to make a bigger plane—which should also fly farther.

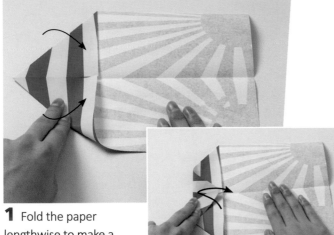

1 Fold the paper lengthwise to make a crease, then open out and fold the corners at one end into the center. Now fold the tip back so that the point lies at the point where the corners meet and make a crease.

2 Turn the nose back and open out one flap, before turning the tip back in. This will begin to reverse the folds of the flap.

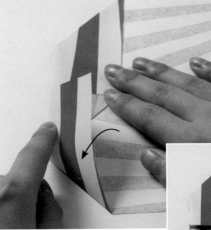

3 Reverse the diagonal crease against the main sheet of paper and bring the corner to lie on the central crease.

4 Open out the flap again to lift the nearer corner up, then repeat the reversal of the creases and flatten.

In the air. Most commercial planes fly at 36,000 feet (11km).

5 Turn the whole paper over and fold the end back on itself.

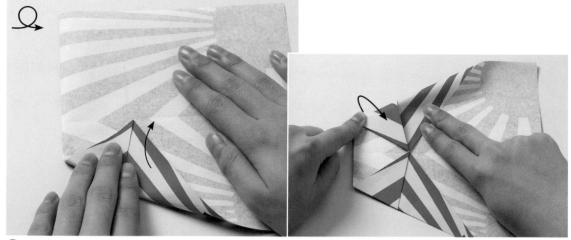

6 Turn the paper back over and turn the two folded corners in at a slight angle so that they meet on the central crease, leaving approximately 2in (5cm) of unturned paper at the far end.

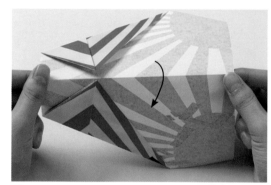

7 Lift the paper up and fold the nearer half behind.

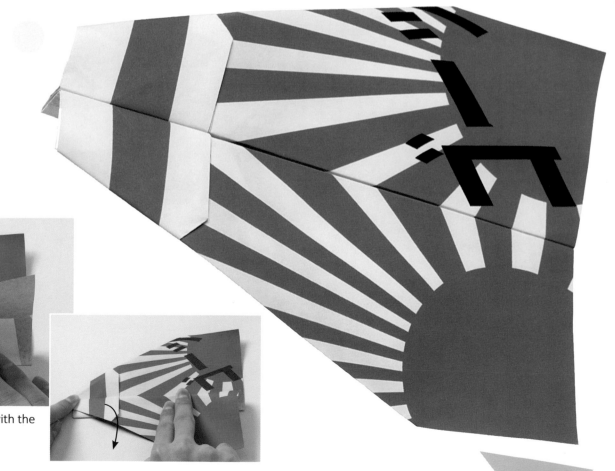

8 Fold down the wings, making the crease parallel with the base of the plane about halfway up the flat nose.

Sparrow

This model is designed to resemble a bird's appearance as it quickly darts through the sky with its small body and large angled wings. The best way to ensure a successful flight is to hold the front part of the airplane between your fingertips and to launch it with a flick of the wrist (see page 7).

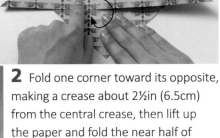

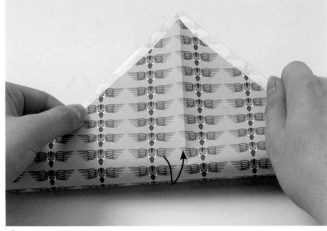

1 Fold the 10in (25cm) square paper in half from corner to corner, then open it out and repeat in the other direction.

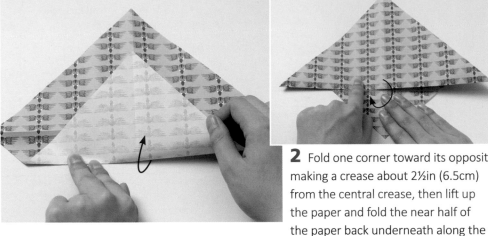

2 Fold one corner toward its opposite, making a crease about 2½in (6.5cm) from the central crease, then lift up the paper and fold the near half of the paper back underneath along the central crease.

3 Turn the paper over, then fold the nearest point back over the previous fold so that it lies on top of the opposite point.

4 Fold the left-hand arm up and over at an angle, using the central crease as the fold point and ensuring that the top left point finishes higher than the top center point of the object.

5 Fold the left-hand side of the paper over using the central crease as the fold line.

High tech! Unmanned aircraft operated remotely are called drones.

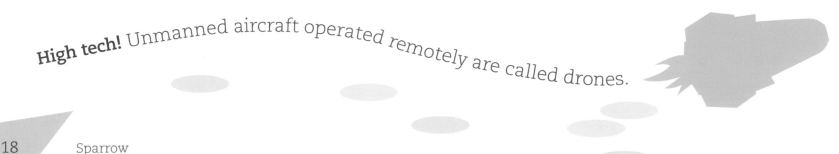

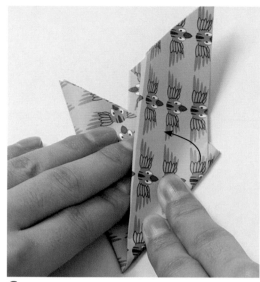

6 Turn over the right-hand arm so that it sits exactly on top of the other one.

7 Open out the object by unfolding the right-hand arm, then refold it so that it sits opposite the other arm.

8 Close up the paper by folding it in half along the central crease.

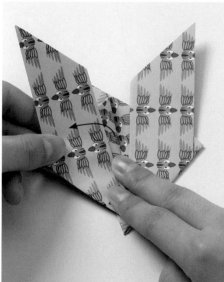

9 Fold back the wing with a new angled crease which also gives the Sparrow a small nose, then turn the object over and repeat on the other side.

10 Finally open out the plane and make its wings even.

X-12

A modern jet fighter, the X-12 was designed to resemble one of the planes seen in popular Japanese cartoons. Its sleek shape and polished look make it perfect for aerial assaults in the backyard. When you are flying your plane with friends, take care not to throw it straight toward them: the point is a bit sharp and a direct hit could hurt them!

1 With the printed side upward, fold the paper in half lengthwise. Next turn down both corners at one end before also turning over the angled edges.

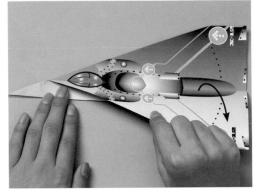

2 Turn over the wing, making the fold along the line of the cockpit so that the designs on both sides of the plane match.

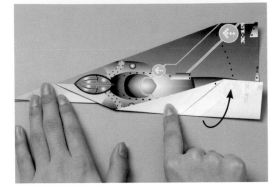

3 Fold back the outer half of the wing, starting the fold line at the edge of the design at the front.

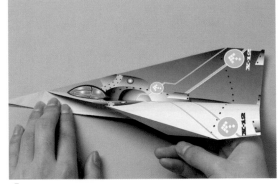

4 Reopen the flap and lift the entire wing, opening out the flap underneath with your fingers.

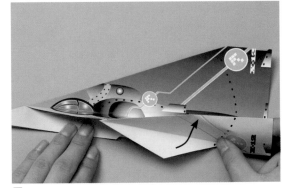

5 Reclose the wing, reversing the diagonal crease.

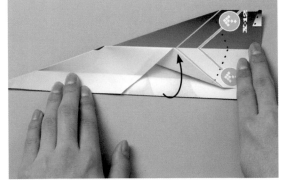

6 Press the wing flat against the other side of the plane and check the folds match the photograph.

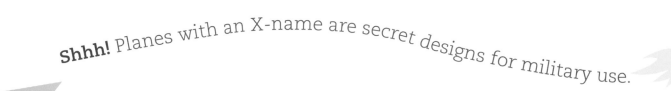

Shhh! Planes with an X-name are secret designs for military use.

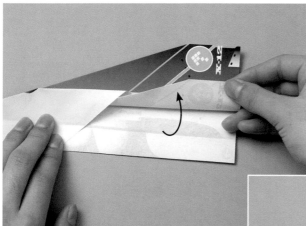

7 Holding the end of the wing in your fingers, turn it upward until the angled edge sits snugly against the inside of the earlier crease. Turn the object over and repeat the last five steps on the other side.

8 Make a long, shallow angled flap at the base of the back of the plane.

9 Open out the plane and reverse the crease from the previous step so that it sticks out above the plane as a tail fin.

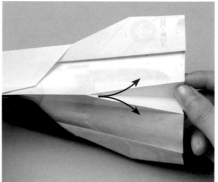

Ross-17

The Ross-17 is taking flight into a new age with a design that will see airplanes flying higher than ever before. This model flies best when the creases are thin and the folds sharp, which will stop the paper around the cockpit from becoming too thick and unwieldy. Take your time, though, as the folds you need to make this plane can be a little complex.

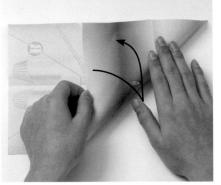

1 First, fold the paper along its length to make a crease and open out. Next fold one corner right across to the other side of the paper to make a diagonal crease and open out before repeating on the other side.

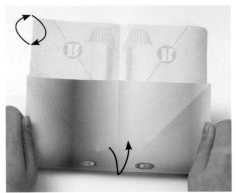

2 Turn over the end of the paper and make a fold where the diagonal creases cross.

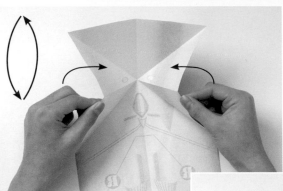

3 Open out the fold and press the two sides together, reversing the horizontal crease so that the sides meet in the center and the end of the paper folds back down to create a triangle.

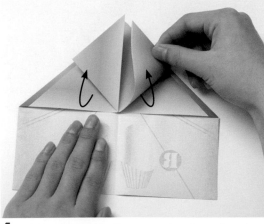

4 Fold back the top flap on each side so that the tips meet at the top of the paper and the edges lie up the central crease.

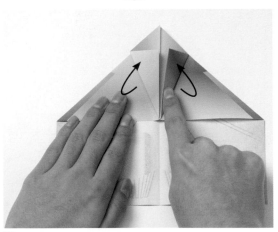

5 Fold in the sides of the diamond so that the edges meet along the middle with the flat edges of the triangles facing forward.

6 Turn back the top layers of the end point and tuck them into the flaps made in the previous step.

Keep out! Planes can't fly into space—the air is too thin to hold them up!

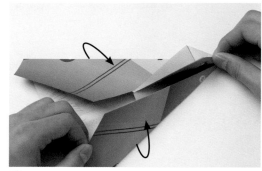

7 Lift up the sides of the diamond and fold the wing in underneath, then let the diamond fall back into place.

8 Turn over the wing tips so that the points lie about 1cm (⅜in) apart directly along the bottom edge of the paper.

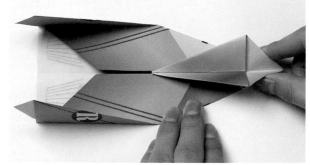

9 Form the wing tips into shape and press up the sides of the diamond so they are angled symmetrically to the plane.

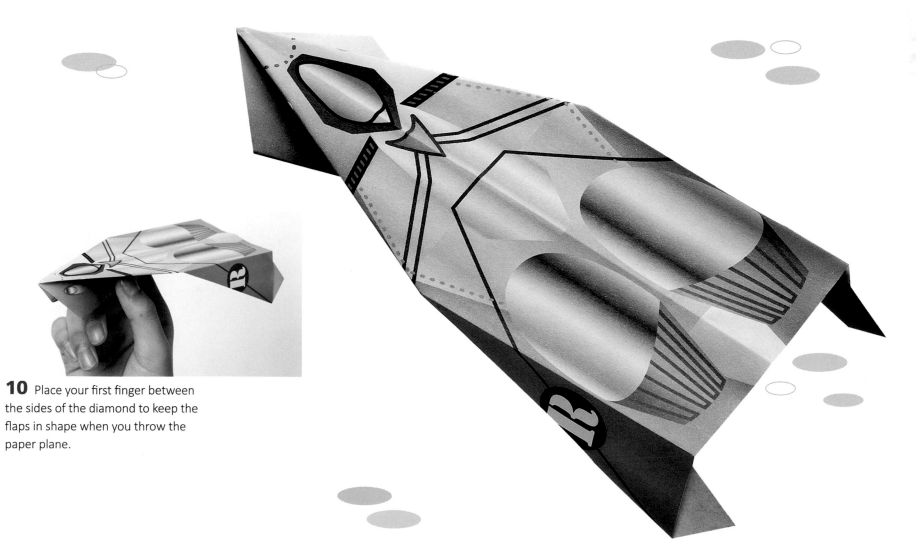

10 Place your first finger between the sides of the diamond to keep the flaps in shape when you throw the paper plane.

Apollo Rocket

The Apollo missions took astronauts to the Moon, farther from Earth than man had ever gone before. This model is made with paper that is a reminder of journeys through space. Although the rocket will not fly, it can be hung on a thread from the ceiling. Perhaps you could fold a series of rockets and pretend they are embarking on intergalactic missions above your head.

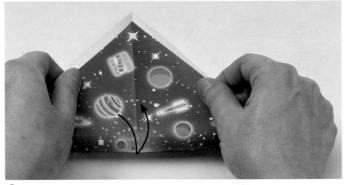

1 Fold the sheet of 10in (25cm) square paper in half to make a crease from corner to corner, then open it and fold in the other direction.

2 Open out and fold one side over to lie on the other and then fold the sheet in half again.

3 Lift the top flap and open out, pressing it down to form a triangle. Turn the sheet over and repeat on the other side.

4 Fold forward the two outer points of the top flap so that they meet at the bottom of the object. Turn the object over and repeat so that you are left with a diamond shape.

5 Spin the object so that the loose points face away from you, then lift the left-hand flap, open it out, and refold into a square. Repeat on the right-hand side.

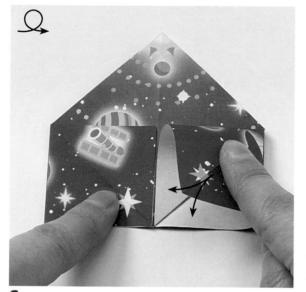

7 Fold the upper left-hand flap to the right, then turn over the object and repeat so that the square flaps made in steps 5 and 6 are hidden inside the object.

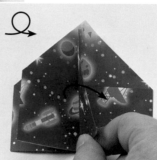

6 Turn the paper over and repeat on the other side.

8 Fold in both sides so that the edges meet along the central crease, then turn the paper over and repeat.

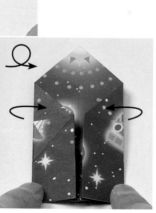

9 Fold the right-hand flap to the left, then turn the paper over and repeat.

Mission accomplished! The Apollo 11 first moon landing was on July 20th 1969.

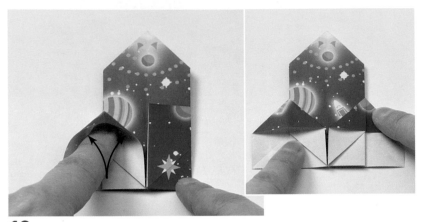

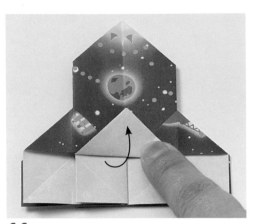

10 Open out the upper left-hand flap, refolding it to form a triangle above a square. Repeat on the right-hand side, then turn the paper over and repeat again.

11 Turn up the triangle that has been left at the bottom in the middle, then turn the object over and repeat.

12 To finish, gently open out the four supports of the rocket so that they are evenly spaced.

Space Shuttle

Your origami journey through space can continue with this realistic model of the Space Shuttle. Simple and quick to make, the shuttle can float above your room like the real thing drifting through space. Imagine looking down on the world you know so well from high above the planet, safe inside the cockpit of the shuttle.

1 With the design side down, fold the sheet of 10in (25cm) square paper in half, then fold both side points up to the top so that the bottom edges meet in the center.

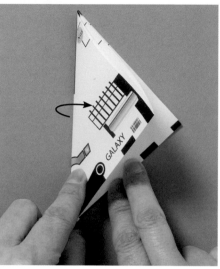

2 Fold the object in half along the vertical center line.

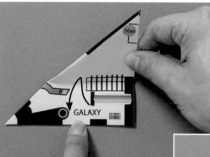

3 Fold down the top point, making a horizontal crease from the top of the space shuttle's windshield, then open up the object and refold the top point inside, reversing the direction of the creases where necessary.

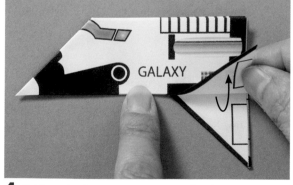

4 Fold up the bottom points to make the wings on both sides of the object.

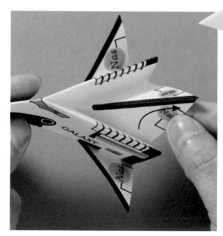

5 Open up the model again and turn up the bottom tip, making new horizontal creases inside that make the tip point straight up as the shuttle's tail.

Hefty! The heaviest space shuttle weighed the same as 13 elephants!

Challenger Rocket

The final model is as close as origami gets to a real rocket—though this does mean it is quite challenging to make. When you have finished folding it, carefully inflate it and then place it on the end of a drinking straw so that it can be launched with one quick breath—can yours replicate the power of the largest rockets and reach the Moon?

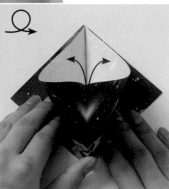

1 Fold the sheet of 10in (25cm) square paper in half from corner to corner, then fold in half again.

2 Lift the top flap, open it out, and refold in a diamond shape by bringing the bottom point up to the top of the paper. Turn the sheet over and repeat.

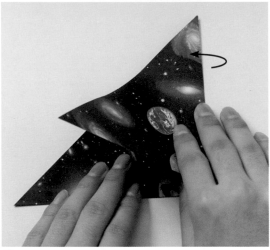

3 Fold the left-hand flap into the center so that the outer edge runs up the middle.

4 Lift up the flap and open it out, refolding it so that it is centered on the paper.

5 Fold the left-hand side of the top flap over, then repeat steps 3 and 4.

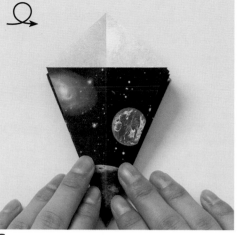

6 Next turn the whole object over and repeat folding in the left-hand flap until you have done it four times in all.

7 Fold forward the top of the object to make a crease, about ½in (1.75cm) under the edge of the visible color on the front of the paper.

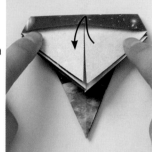

8 Turn the top flap on the right-hand side over to the left.

9 Fold forward the upper flap along the crease made in step 7 and flatten the two central pieces that are sticking up.

Zoom! Rockets can travel at 22,000mph (35,000kph).

10 Turn the object over, fold the right-hand flap to the left before once again folding the top forward and flattening.

11 Again turn the right-hand flap to the left and fold forward the top flap.

12 Fold over three flaps so that the last remaining tall flap is uppermost, then turn down the top point in the same way.

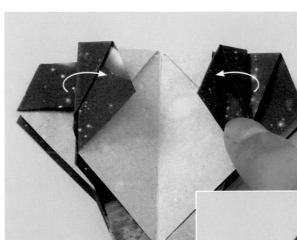

13 Reform the object so that there are two flaps on each side, then fold in the sides of each flap to make winglets.

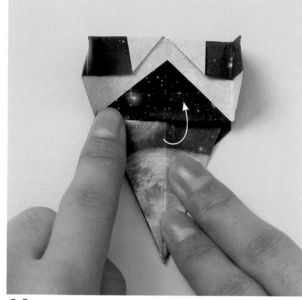

14 Turn over the loose triangle of paper inside each flap so that it is flush with the winglets.

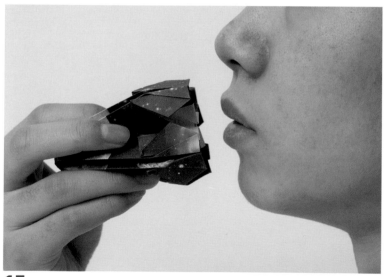

15 Gently open out the flaps and, holding them apart in your fingers, carefully blow into the hole at the base of the object to give it shape.

About the authors

Mari Ono is an expert in origami and all forms of papercrafts. Born in Japan, she has lived in the UK for many years with her artist husband, Takumasa, where they both work to promote Japanese arts and crafts. Her other books include the best-selling *The Simple Art of Origami, Origami for Children, More Origami for Children, How to Make Paper Planes and Other Flying Objects, Wild and Wonderful Origami, Origami for Mindfulness,* and *Origami Farm,* all available from CICO Books.

Roshin Ono moved to the UK from Japan at the age of seven with his mother Mari, a graphic designer, and artist father. He has participated in events introducing Japanese culture to the western world as well as writing *Origami for Children* with his mother.

Suppliers

Origami paper is available at most good paper stores or online. Try searching online for "origami paper" to find a whole range of stores, selling a wide variety of paper, that will send packages directly to your home.

UK
HOBBYCRAFT
www.hobbycraft.co.uk
TEL: +44 (0)330 026 1400

JP-BOOKS
www.jpbooks.co.uk
TEL: +44 (0)20 7839 4839
info@jpbooks.co.uk

JAPAN CENTRE
www.japancentre.com
TEL: +44 (0)20 3405 1151
enquiry@japancentre.com

THE JAPANESE SHOP
www.thejapaneseshop.co.uk
info@thejapaneseshop.co.uk

USA
A.C. MOORE
www.acmoore.com
Stores nationwide
TEL: 1-888-226-6673

HOBBY LOBBY
www.hobbylobby.com
Stores nationwide

JO-ANN FABRIC AND CRAFT STORE
www.joann.com
Stores nationwide
TEL: 1-888-739-4120

MICHAELS STORES
www.michaels.com
Stores nationwide
TEL: 1-800-642-4235

HAKUBUNDO (HONOLULU, HAWAII)
www.hakubundo.com
TEL: (808) 947-5503
web@hakubundo.com

Note: All the models are made from square paper except for Star Strike, Star Light, Thunderstorm, Sunlight, X-12, and Ross-17, which are made from 6in x 9½in (170 x 241mm) paper. You only need one sheet for each project, but there is additional paper to make two Classic Planes, Gliders, Sparrows, Apollo Rockets, Space Shuttles, and Challenger Rockets.

18 sheets of origami paper

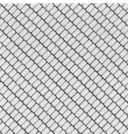
1. Classic Plane

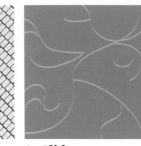
2. Glider

3. Star Strike

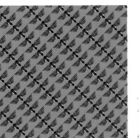
4. Star Light

5. Thunderstorm

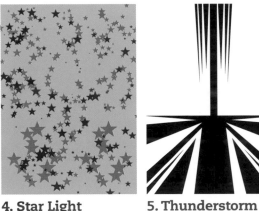
6. Sunlight

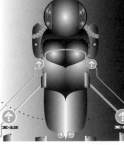
7. Sparrow

8. X-12

9. Ross-17

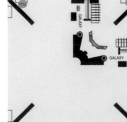
10. Apollo Rocket

11. Space Shuttle

12. Challenger

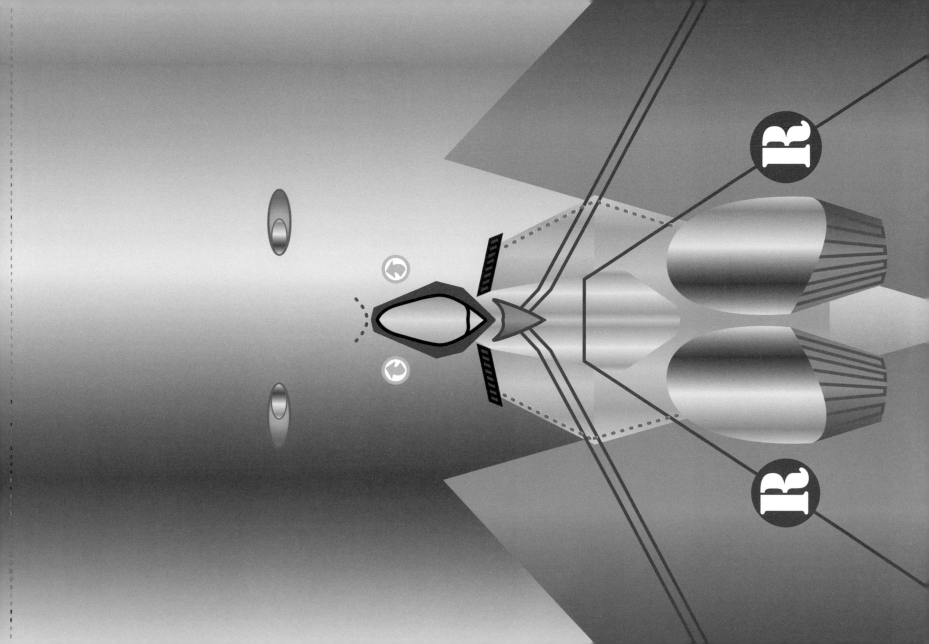

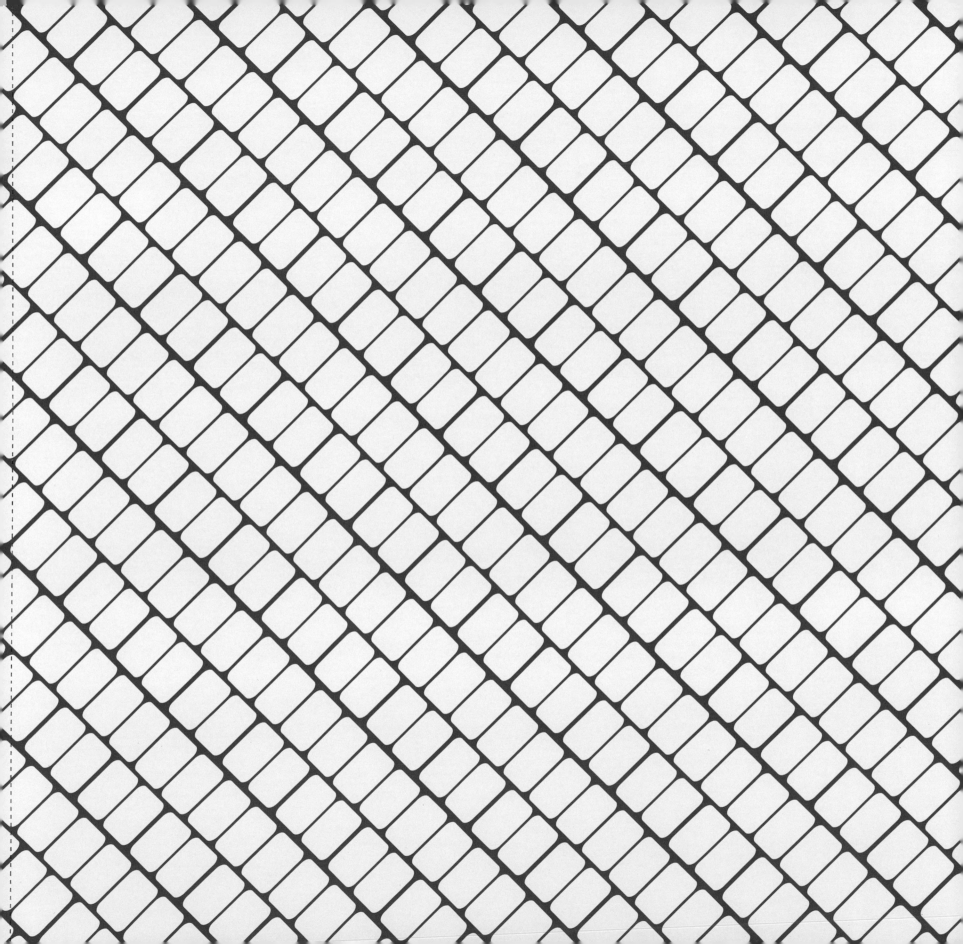

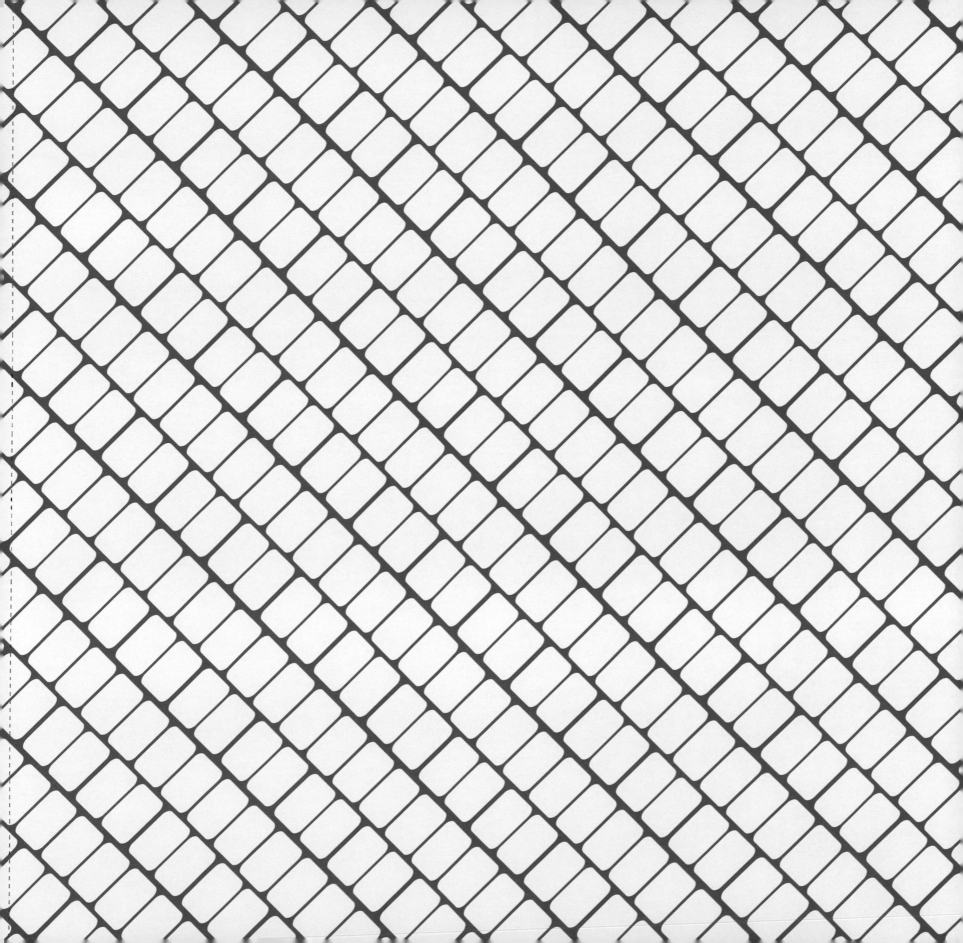

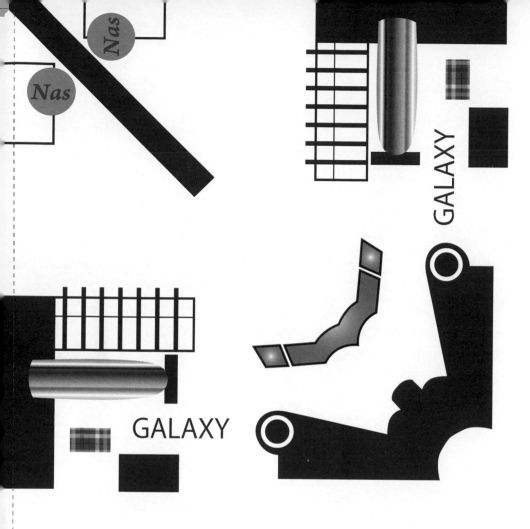

GALAXY

GALAXY

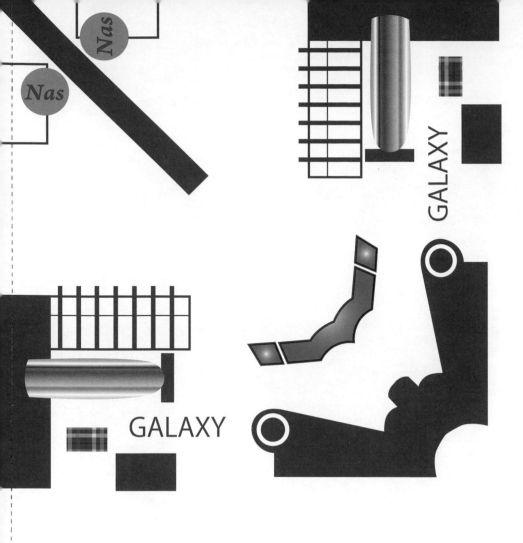

GALAXY

GALAXY